The Heights of Macchu Picchu

Alturas de Macchu Picchu /

THE HEIGHTS OF

NEW YORK

Pablo Neruda

MACCHU PICCHU

Translated by Nathaniel Tarn

FARRAR, STRAUS & GIROUX

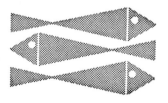

This edition © 1966 by Jonathan Cape Ltd.

Translation © 1966 by Nathaniel Tarn

Preface © 1966 by Robert Pring-Mill

All rights reserved

Fourth printing, 1971

Library of Congress catalog card number: 67–15010

Printed in the United States of America

Designed by Guy Fleming

I AM INCALCULABLY GRATEFUL TO MR. ROBERT PRING-MILL, FELLOW of St. Catherine's College, Oxford, for his warmth, tact, and great patience in helping me with this translation. His deep familiarity with Neruda's work allowed me to see the structure of the poem far more clearly than I would have done unaided, and many of his suggestions were incorporated into the final version. Mr. J. M. Cohen and Dr. George Steiner were also kind enough to give me some valuable advice. At a late stage in the drafting, I studied with profit and interest a number of available versions, including those of Messrs. Roger Caillois and Rudolf Hagelstange.

Señor Neruda helped me with a number of problems of interpretation by correspondence from his home in Isla Negra. I have based myself, at his suggestion, on the text of the latest edition of Obras Completas (1962), but I have followed some aspects of the spacing in the text printed in Himno y Regreso (1948) where it seemed to me to clarify certain matters and to help the reader in following a very complex poem. Although English and American *sources spell the name of the site as Machu Picchu, I have, for the sake of consistency, followed Neruda's spelling everywhere: Macchu Picchu.*

I would like to dedicate this version of The Heights of Macchu Picchu *to my wife Patricia and to Señora Neruda.*

NATHANIEL TARN

Preface

NERUDA IS ONE OF THE GREATEST POETS writing in Spanish today, and *The Heights of Macchu Picchu* is his finest poem. He made his name over forty years ago, with his second book, *Veinte poemas de amor y una canción desesperada* (1924), which has sold over one and a quarter million copies in the Spanish text alone—and goes on selling. Born in 1904 in Parral, in the south of Chile (son of a crew foreman on the Chilean railways), he spent most of his childhood in the small provincial town of Temuco. His real name was Neftalí Reyes, but fear of ridicule from his relations made him use a pseudonym, which he coined by borrowing the exotic surname of a nineteenth-century Czech writer and changing "Neftalí" to "Pablo." His early poetry brought him swift success among his fellow students in Santiago, but it was the *Veinte poemas* which gained him wider fame, with its brilliant use of a close-knit web of nature symbolism to define and analyze his personal response to experience.

Like other Latin American countries, Chile sometimes honors her poets by giving them a diplomatic post, and in 1927 Neruda was sent as consul to Rangoon. He spent the next five years in various consulates in Southeast Asia, and during this time a sense of isolation which had already marked the earlier love poetry grew into a desolate bleakness, under the pressure of two alien cultures: that of the indigenous Asiatic peoples, with whom he could make little intellectual contact, and that of the European merchants and colonial administrators with whom he had to deal. His poetry turned tortuously in upon itself, displaying resentment and disgust at every form of city life, whose routine emptiness oppressed him as much in Asia as it had done in Santiago. The inherited world-picture went to pieces around him, and Neruda mirrored its collapse in a meticulous disintegration of traditional poetic forms. His poems became series of seemingly random metaphorical approximations to clear statement, organized into a studied semblance of "chaos" around a central core of emotion. Some of this poetry (collected in the two volumes of *Residencia en la tierra,* 1933 and 1935) is extremely obscure, largely due to his use of private symbols under the influence of the Surrealists, and it reflects the consciousness of spiritual sterility one finds in so many poets between 1918 and 1936.

He was transferred to Barcelona in 1934, and to Madrid the following February. The outbreak of the Spanish civil war in July 1936, together with García Lorca's murder, shattered the mood of introspection which had produced the poems of *Residencia en la tierra.* Hitherto a somewhat romantic anarchist, he became a Communist supporter (although he did not join the party until nine years later). His first volume of "committed" poetry (*España en el corazón,* 1937) had a stark directness and a strident note absent from everything he had previously written. He spent the civil-war years helping the Republican cause—in Spain, France, and Chile— later going back to Europe to organize the emigration of Spanish Republican refugees to Latin America. In August 1940, he was appointed Chilean consul-general in Mexico.

Neruda held this post for just over three years, during which his reputation steadily grew. His return to Chile in October 1943 was a triumphal journey, on which he found himself acclaimed in capital after capital by huge crowds for whom his poetry seemed to voice the sufferings and aspirations of all the Latin American peoples. It was during this journey that Neruda made the trip to Macchu Picchu which inspired the poem he wrote almost two years later, in September 1945. Its central symbol is the ascent to the ruins of this lost Inca city high up in the Peruvian Andes, whose very existence was unknown till 1911, though it is barely eighty miles from Cuzco.

Cuzco had been the Inca capital, center of an empire stretching three thousand miles from north to south, with a very highly developed civilization and a complex social structure. A few miles northeast of Cuzco stands Pisac, a fortress city on a massive pinnacle of rock, guarding the upper Urubamba. From Pisac, the river surges on through the craggy gorges of a winding V-shaped valley toward the distant basin of the Amazon, with a whole system of fortress sanctuaries—once linked by a stone-built road—set on the heights from fifteen hundred to two thousand feet above the Urubamba, and about ten miles apart: Ollantaytambo (still under construction when the Spaniards came in 1536), Huamanmarca, Patallacta, Winay-whayna, Botamarca, and Loyamarca. There, as far as anybody knew for centuries, the series ended. Farther downstream, however, stood the most spectacular of all these cities: set high between two peaks, to overlook the place where the Urubamba goes cascading into humid jungles and to protect the highway to the capital from their untamed tribes.

The peaks are Macchu Picchu and Huayna Picchu—Old and New Picchu—and the former gave its name to the citadel which stands in the saddle between them, when Hiram Bingham found it at a time when Neruda was a boy of seven, down south in Temuco. A "tall city of stepped stone" [VI], Macchu Picchu stands in a grandiose setting, clinging to its geometrically terraced slope above the swirling river, among enormous mountains—their lower reaches and the lesser peaks all densely forested. Except for the absence of its straw-thatched roofs, the unpeopled city is intact: intricately patterned, with terraces, watercourses, squares, temples, and the high-gabled walls of empty houses interlocking to form a single architectural complex—planned as a unit, and built by collective labor. It is an abstract composition: a pattern of right angles and perpendiculars and horizontals, with slanting stairs and gable ends and the typical Inca trapezoidal doors and gates and niches, without a curve save where walls bend. The structure has an almost crystalline appearance, its rectilinear symmetries giving an impression of immutability—polished by the winds, but otherwise unchanged since its inhabitants abandoned it for no known reason and at an unknown date.

In the poem which Neruda wrote about the ruins, this citadel becomes the center of a tangled skein of associations with disparate and intertwining strands. It is by no means a clear-cut symbol, because its meaning shifts as the strong current of emotion winds between past and present, but Neruda's journey gradually takes on the nature of a highly personal "venture to the interior" in which he explores both his own inner world and the past of Latin American man. There is no explicit mention of the city till the sixth of the twelve poems which form the sequence, its earlier sections dealing not with Neruda's physical journey but with a kind of pilgrimage through human life in search of meaningful truth. When Neruda does reach Macchu Picchu, its heights turn out to be the place from which all else makes sense, including his own continent.

In *The Heights of Macchu Picchu,* Neruda's earlier work falls into place. Its first five poems are almost a recapitulatory survey of the different moods and settings of his previous poetry, whose various strands he weaves into a single complex fabric. In this, he makes repeated use of the whole range of heightened meanings with which he had endowed his major themes and images: earth and sea, the air; the fecund cycle of the seasons and the renewal of nature; the tree as an image of mankind and man; grain and bread, sexual love; irresistible Death, and the humiliating petty deaths and diminutions of humdrum urban life; the transience of the individual seen against the expanse of time; life as a rushing torrent; the experience of chaos and the hunger to discern some principle of order; the pointless surface of existence and the search for meaning; isolation among one's fellows, and the longing to "communicate" and thus discover some significant identity defined by a reciprocal relationship. These images are profoundly disturbing, whether or not one understands the details of Neruda's personal cosmology or shares his views on man, and the poem takes on a special meaning for each reader in terms of his response to his own experience.

This is in one sense true of any poem, yet the range of one's freedom of response is far more rigidly controlled by poems with an explicit line of argument. Neruda works with ambiguities, not stating but suggesting, and usually suggesting a number of different lines of thought and feeling at any given time. It is this feature of his approach which makes his poetry so extraordinarily hard to translate, and he exploits the full range of ambiguity by means of numerous technical devices. Thus, no sooner has the sequence opened than it moves into a web of two-way syntax that creates conflicting patterns of association around the imagery. Ambiguous syntax is one of the most fascinating aspects of Neruda's manner of proceeding in all his complex poems, yet it is a feature which is peculiarly tantalizing to translators. They can rarely hope to establish a corresponding ambiguity, and therefore have either to opt between layers of meaning, or else to give the grammatical sense of a single layer while trying to suggest the others by words which carry heightened and conflicting associations, as Tarn does. Sometimes, too, a word will have to be intensified because of a degree of abstraction which seems nebulous in English, requiring some kind of concrete rendering to achieve an equivalent impact: this is particularly true of some very frequent terms like *vacío*, or *manantiales*, or *diseminado*, and Neruda's thinking is not necessarily imprecise because such terms seem vague. He has very often taken a fairly neutral word and loaded it with his own associations by using it in numerous previous contexts, whose cumulative effect has been to extend and clarify its field of meaning: such terms cannot always be translated here by a single intensified equivalent, since different shades of meaning have to be brought out in different contexts. A further difficulty lies in the fact that Neruda's poetry has a natural setting whose grandeur obliges a translator to work close to the brink of what might seem hyperbole—a danger Tarn tries to avoid by using taut-phrased, sharp-edged images wherever possible.

The first poem of the sequence opens with the image of an empty net, "dredging through streets and ambient atmosphere," sifting experience but gathering nothing. This opening section shows us Neruda drained by the surface of existence, seeking inwards and downwards for a hidden "vein of gold"; then sinking lower still, through the waves of a symbolic sea, in a blind search to rediscover "the jasmine of our exhausted human spring"—an erotic symbol, tinged by its contextual imagery with the associations of a vanished paradise, and leading us like Eliot's *Burnt Norton* back "through the first gate" and "into our first world."

The second poem contrasts the enduring values of self-perpetuating nature, as rich and fecund in the rocks as in the seed, with man grinding things down until he finds his own soul left impoverished. It shows us the poet longing for time to stand and stare and thus to find his way back to the kind of truth he had "fingered once in stone," or experienced in the lightning flash released by love (the source of such urgent beauty in the *Veinte poemas*). This kind of truth endures in grain, as well as in the "ghost of home in the translucent water": water, perpetually flowing from the Andes down to the Pacific, is a constant feature of Neruda's Chilean background, taking on symbolic overtones in his poetry that go far beyond the traditional Spanish equation between men's lives and rivers which flow steadily toward the sea of death. Such truth cannot be found, however, in the cluster of men's empty faces: in city life—all shops and stores and factory whistles, mankind reduced to robotlike automata—there seems to be no trace of the undying "quality of life" in which Neruda still believes. Where then can it be found? That question stays unanswered for three further poems, devoted to considering the nature of two facets of death: one great and noble, and (like the "quality of life") not to be found in cities; the other a gradual and humiliating process.

The latter is the subject of the third poem, which looks directly at modern man's existence: seeing it husked off the cob like maize and settling into the granary of mean events, as each individual is whittled away by routine living—not proudly scythed at a single stroke. Urban men wilt slowly away: Neruda regards their kind of life as a wasting death in a black cup, filled with hardship, illness, toil, and loneliness. This image of the black cup, trembling—because they tremble—as they tip it back, prepares the way for the contrasting image of Macchu Picchu as a "permanence of stone . . . raised like a chalice" [VII]. The religious overtones of such an image seem quite deliberate, and I think that Neruda often uses Christian imagery (part of the general Catholic heritage of South America) to heighten a vital point much as Renaissance poets used the pagan myths, bringing the textured associations of an extended frame of reference into play without implying the literal truth of its conceptual framework.

The fourth poem takes us a stage further, not only showing Neruda wooed by the greater Death (using sea imagery to hint at its attraction) but also introducing the theme of love for the poet's fellow men. This remains unrealizable, however, as long as all he sees of them is just their daily death: his own experience in the urban context progressively closes him off from them, driving him street by street to the last degrading hovel where he has to face his own small death, in an empty mood which recalls the desolation of *Residencia en la tierra*. The short fifth poem defines this kind of death even more closely in a series of seemingly surrealistic images, leaving a final vision of modern life with nothing in its wounds "save wind in gusts," to chill one's "cold interstices of soul." At that point, the tide is at the ebb: this is the lowest, coldest stage of the whole sequence.

Then, quite suddenly, the poem begins to rise (in the sixth section) as Neruda climbs upward in space toward the heights of Macchu Picchu and backward in time toward the moment when that geometrically perfect city was created: a moment in time which is a point where all lines come together, things click abruptly into place, and the pattern of past and present suddenly makes sense—a sense which will later turn out to contain built-in lessons for the future (but these are not immediately made clear, perhaps not even seen yet by the poet). Here, "two lineages that had run parallel" meet and fuse: the line behind small men and petty deaths and the line of permanence behind the recurring fertility of nature have been produced into the past, as it were, until they paradoxically met at one still point which *"was* the habitation . . . *is* the site"—resembling the "still point of the turning world" where "past and future are gathered," in *Burnt Norton.*

Macchu Picchu is the place where "maize grew high" and where men carded the vicuña's fleece to weave royal robes and both funereal and festive garments. What endures is the collective permanence those men created: all that was transitory has disappeared, leaving the stone city to the lustration of the air. Section VII picks up this contrast between what endures and what has vanished, and sees "the true, the most consuming death" (which Neruda could not find in modern streets) as having slain those long-past men— their death being nobler because it was a collective experience (they are the "shades of one ravine" who "plummeted like an autumn into a single death"). What they left behind them was their citadel— "raised like a chalice in all those hands"—which Neruda sees as "the everlasting rose, our home" (*la rosa permanente, la morada*). This "rose" is one of Neruda's favorite symbols, taken up in the *Oda al edificio* (*Odas elementales,* 1954) in a way which seems to me to illuminate its meaning here: in the later poem, men have to overcome all petty prides so as to build a dome—a deft balancing of calculated forces—thereby bringing order out of the various materials which they have taken from nature, in the erection of "the collective rose" which is "the edifice of all mankind," structured on reason and steel in the pursuit of happiness. The implications of the "everlasting rose" in *Macchu Picchu* are not yet as clear-cut, but it points in this direction.

Neruda feels that he can "identify" with the absolute Death he finds on the heights, but his search for this true death has been a search for a more positive kind of identity as well, and also for identification through nature with his fellow men. The journey backward in time and upward in space was an exploration in which the poet learned—more by means of feeling than by means of thought—to see new facets of the truth, both about himself and about the nature of existence. The journey does not end, however, at this still point, with the discovery of the city living its enduring "life of stone." There is already a hint of the final outcome in "life of stone *after so many lives,*" but the buoyancy of his discovery lasts through the next two poems: VIII, with its vivid evocation of surging nature and pre-Columbian man linked in their common dawn, and fused together by a warm instinctive love which the poet summons up from the past to transfuse the present and embrace the future (anticipating the more personal summons to his past "brothers" in XI) ; and IX, a solemn and incantatory chant made up of units based on interlocking metaphors, with the phrase *de piedra* ("of stone") recurring like the "Ora pro nobis" of a litany, building up to a final pair of lines which brings us starkly back both to the great mass of men who raised the citadel and to the one-way thrust of man-slaying time.

The poem's last major turning point comes with the question opening its tenth section: "Stone within stone, and man, where was he?" Neruda begins to wonder whether the men who built up stone on stone, in long-past time, may not perhaps have been like urban man today, and whether the geometrical precision of the citadel might not in fact have been erected on a base of human suffering: "stone above stone on a groundwork of rags." If built by slaves, in what conditions did these live? Was Ancient America— that not only "bore the rose in mind" but could translate it "into the radiant weave of matter"—based on starvation, hoarding "the eagle hunger" in its depths?

In the eleventh section, Neruda strives to get beyond the weave of matter until he can hold "the old and unremembered human heart" in his hand (feeling it pulse like a captive bird), seeing behind the "transcendental span" of Macchu Picchu to the invisible "hypotenuse of hairshirt and salt blood" implied by each right angle in those ruins. Man is what matters because "man is wider than all the sea," and Neruda wants to get through to all the men who died building this city, so that they may rise again to birth—with him and through him—as his "brothers." It would be easy to smile at this in the light of other prejudices, seeing it as a kind of futile retroactive "Workers of the world, unite!" But the moral it draws from the past thrusts forward in the same direction as devouring time, and the Neruda who summons the vanished craftsmen of Macchu Picchu in the final poem, asking them to show him the places of their agony (evoked in language linking their sufferings to the stations of the Cross), is a noble and imposing figure, who finds his ultimate fulfillment in becoming the valid spokesman of the dead—of his South American dead in particular, but in the last resort, of all mankind.

What really matters to Neruda now is that which his own experience has in common with the experience of other men, plus the urgency of his need to show men to themselves in such a way that they can feel the identity behind their separate lives, and share his insight. Yet on its way toward this "public" ending, the sequence has explored numerous more private interpenetrating layers of human existence, and the force of its discoveries at these different levels lingers on despite the public nature of the resolution.

ROBERT PRING-MILL

St. Catherine's College,
Oxford

I

DEL AIRE AL AIRE, *como una red vacía,*
iba yo entre las calles y la atmósfera, llegando y despidiendo,
en el advenimiento del otoño la moneda extendida
de las hojas, y, entre la primavera y las espigas,
lo que el más grande amor, como dentro de un guante
que cae, nos entrega como una larga luna.

(Días de fulgor vivo en la intemperie
de los cuerpos: aceros convertidos
al silencio del ácido:
noches deshilachadas hasta la última harina:
estambres agredidos de la patria nupcial.)

Alguien que me esperó entre los violines
encontró un mundo como una torre enterrada
hundiendo su espiral más abajo de todas
las hojas de color de ronco azufre:
más abajo, en el oro de la geología,
como una espada envuelta en meteoros,
hundí la mano turbulenta y dulce
en lo más genital de lo terrestre.

Puse la frente entre las olas profundas,
descendí como gota entre la paz sulfúrica,
y, como un ciego, regresé al jazmín
de la gastada primavera humana.

From air to air, like an empty net,
dredging through streets and ambient atmosphere, I came
lavish, at autumn's coronation, with the leaves'
proffer of currency and—between spring and wheat ears—
that which a boundless love, caught in a gauntlet fall,
grants us like a long-fingered moon.

(Days of live radiance in discordant
bodies: steels converted
to the silence of acid:
nights disentangled to the ultimate flour,
assaulted stamens of the nuptial land.)

Someone waiting for me among the violins
met with a world like a buried tower
sinking its spiral below the layered leaves
color of raucous sulphur:
and lower yet, in a vein of gold,
like a sword in a scabbard of meteors,
I plunged a turbulent and tender hand
to the most secret organs of the earth.

Leaning my forehead through unfathomed waves
I sank, a single drop, within a sleep of sulphur
where, like a blind man, I retraced the jasmine
of our exhausted human spring.

II

Sɪ ʟᴀ ꜰʟᴏʀ *a la flor entrega el alto germen*
y la roca mantiene su flor diseminada
en su golpeado traje de diamante y arena,
el hombre arruga el pétalo de la luz que recoge
en los determinados manantiales marinos
y taladra el metal palpitante en sus manos.
Y pronto, entre la ropa y el humo, sobre la mesa hundida,
como una barajada cantidad, queda el alma:
cuarzo y desvelo, lágrimas en el océano
como estanques de frío: pero aún
mátala y agonízala con papel y con odio,
sumérgela en la alfombra cotidiana, desgárrala
entre las vestiduras hostiles del alambre.

No: por los corredores, aire, mar o caminos,
quién guarda sin puñal (como las encarnadas
amapolas) su sangre? La cólera ha extenuado
la triste mercancía del vendedor de seres,
y, mientras en la altura del ciruelo, el rocío
desde mil años deja su carta trasparente
sobre la misma rama que lo espera, oh corazón, oh frente triturada
entre las cavidades del otoño.

Cuántas veces en las calles de invierno de una ciudad o en
un autobús o un barco en el crepúsculo, o en la soledad
más espesa, la de la noche de fiesta, bajo el sonido

FLOWER to flower delivers up its seed
and rock maintains its blossom broadcast
in a bruised garment of diamond and sand
yet man crumples the petal of the light he skims
from the predetermined sources of the sea
and drills the pulsing metal in his hands.
Soon, caught between clothes and smoke, on the sunken floor,
the soul's reduced to a shuffled pack,
quartz and insomnia, tears in the sea,
like pools of cold—yet this is not enough:
he kills, confesses it on paper with contempt,
muffles it in the rug of habit, shreds it
in a hostile apparel of wire.

No: for in corridors—air, sea or land—
who guards his veins unarmed
like scarlet poppies? Now rage has bled
the dreary wares of the trader in creatures,
while, in the plum tree's coronet, the dew
has left a coat of visitations for a thousand years
pinned to the waiting twig, oh heart, oh face
ground small among the cavities of autumn.

How many times in wintry city streets, or in
a bus, a boat at dusk, or in the denser solitude
of festive nights, drenched in the sound

de sombras y campanas, en la misma gruta del placer humano,
me quise detener a buscar la eterna veta insondable
que antes toqué en la piedra o en el relámpago que el beso
    desprendía.

(Lo que en el cereal como una historia amarilla
de pequeños pechos preñados va repitiendo un número
que sin cesar es ternura en las capas germinales,
y que, idéntica siempre, se desgrana en marfil
y lo que en el agua es patria transparente, campana
desde la nieve aislada hasta las olas sangrientas.)

No pude asir sino un racimo de rostros o de máscaras
precipitadas, como anillos de oro vacío,
como ropas dispersas hijas de un otoño rabioso
que hiciera temblar el miserable árbol de las razas asustadas.

No tuve sitio donde descansar la mano
y que, corriente como agua de manantial encadenado,
o firme como grumo de antracita o cristal,
hubiera devuelto el calor o el frío de mi mano extendida.

Qué era el hombre? En qué parte de su conversación abierta
entre los almacenes y los silbidos, en cuál de sus movimientos
    metálicos
vivía lo indestructible, lo imperecedero, la vida?

of bells and shadows, in the very lair of human pleasure,
have I wanted to pause and look for the eternal, unfathomable
truth's filament I'd fingered once in stone, or in the flash a kiss
    released.

(That which in wheat like yellow history
of small, full breasts repeats a calculus
ceaselessly tender in the burgeoning
and which, always the same way, husks to ivory—
that which is ghost of home in the translucent water
belling from the lone snows down to these waves of blood.)

I could only grasp a cluster of faces or masks
thrown down like rings of hollow gold,
like scarecrow clothes, daughters of rabid autumn
shaking the stunted tree of the frightened races.

I had no place in which my hand could rest—
no place running like harnessed water,
firm as a nugget of anthracite or crystal—
responding, hot or cold, to my open hand.

What was man? In what layer of his humdrum conversation,
among his shops and sirens—in which of his metallic movements
lived on imperishably the quality of life?

III

EL SER COMO *el maíz se desgranaba en el inacabable*
granero de los hechos perdidos, de los acontecimientos
miserables, del uno al siete, al ocho,
y no una muerte, sino muchas muertes, llegaba a cada uno:
cada día una muerte pequeña, polvo, gusano, lámpara
que se apaga en el lodo del suburbio, una pequeña muerte
*   de alas gruesas*
entraba en cada hombre como una corta lanza
y era el hombre asediado del pan o del cuchillo,
el ganadero: el hijo de los puertos, o el capitán oscuro del arado,
o el roedor de las calles espesas:

todos desfallecieron esperando su muerte, su corta
*   muerte diaria:*
y su quebranto aciago de cada día era
como una copa negra que bebían temblando.

Bᴇɪɴɢ ʟɪᴋᴇ maize grains fell
in the inexhaustible store of lost deeds, shoddy
occurrences, from nine to five, to six,
and not one death but many came to each,
each day a little death: dust, maggot, lamp,
drenched in the mire of suburbs, a little death with fat wings
entered into each man like a short blade
and siege was laid to him by bread or knife:
the drover, the son of harbors, the dark captain of plows,
the rodent wanderer through dense streets;

all of them weakened waiting for their death, their brief
        and daily death—
and their ominous dwindling each day
was like a black cup they trembled while they drained.

IV

L<small>A PODEROSA</small> *muerte me invitó muchas veces:*
era como la sal invisible en las olas,
y lo que su invisible sabor diseminaba
era como mitades de hundimientos y altura
o vastas construcciones de viento y ventisquero.

Yo al férreo filo vine, a la angostura
del aire, a la mortaja de agricultura y piedra,
al estelar vacío de los pasos finales
y a la vertiginosa carretera espiral:
pero, ancho mar, oh muerte!, de ola en ola no vienes,
sino como un galope de claridad nocturna
o como los totales números de la noche.

Nunca llegaste a hurgar en el bolsillo, no era
posible tu visita sin vestimenta roja:
sin auroral alfombra de cercado silencio:
sin altos o enterrados patrimonios de lágrimas.

No pude amar en cada ser un árbol
con su pequeño otoño a cuestas (la muerte
*   de mil hojas),*
todas las falsas muertes y las resurrecciones
sin tierra, sin abismo:
quise nadar en las más anchas vidas,
en las más sueltas desembocaduras,

IRRESISTIBLE death invited me many times:
it was like salt occulted in the waves
and what its invisible fragrance suggested
was fragments of wrecks and heights
or vast structures of wind and snowdrift.

I had come to the cut of the blade, the narrowest
channel in air, the shroud of field and stone,
the interstellar void of ultimate steps
and the awesome spiral way:
though not through wave on wave do you attain us, vast sea of death,
but rather like a gallop of twilight,
the comprehensive mathematics of the dark.

You never came to scrabble in our pockets,
you could not pay a visit without a scarlet mantle,
an early carpet hush enclosed in silence,
a heritage of tears, enshrined or buried here.

I could not love within each man a tree
with its remaindered autumns on its back (leaves falling
    in their thousands),
all these false deaths and all these resurrections,
sans earth, sans depths:
I wished to swim in the most ample lives,
the widest estuaries,

y cuando poco a poco el hombre fué negándome
y fué cerrando paso y puerto para que no tocaran
mis manos manantiales su inexistencia herida,
entonces fuí por calle y calle y río y río,
y ciudad y ciudad y cama y cama,
y atravesó el desierto mi máscara salobre,
y en las últimas casas humilladas, sin lámpara, sin fuego,
sin pan, sin piedra, sin silencio, solo,
rodé muriendo de mi propia muerte.

and when, little by little, man came denying me
closing his paths and doors so that I could not touch
his wounded inexistence with my divining fingers,
I came by other ways, through streets, river by river,
city by city, one bed after another,
forcing my brackish semblance through a wilderness
till in the last of hovels, lacking all light and fire,
bread, stone and silence, I paced at last alone,
dying of my own death.

V

No ERAS TÚ, *muerte grave, ave de plumas férreas,*
la que el pobre heredero de las habitaciones
llevaba entre alimentos apresurados, bajo la piel vacía:
era algo, un pobre pétalo de cuerda exterminada:
un átomo del pecho que no vino al combate
o el áspero rocío que no cayó en la frente.
Era lo que no pudo renacer, un pedazo
de la pequeña muerte sin paz ni territorio:
un hueso, una campana que morían en él.

Yo levanté las vendas del yodo, hundí las manos
en los pobres dolores que mataban la muerte,
y no encontré en la herida sino una racha fría
que entraba por los vagos intersticios del alma.

It was not you, grave death, raptor of iron plumage,
that the drab tenant of such lodgings carried
mixed with his gobbled rations under hollow skin—
rather: a trodden tendril of old rope,
the atom of a courage that gave way
or some harsh dew never distilled to sweat.
This could not be reborn, a particle
of death without a requiem,
bare bone or fading church bell dying from within.

Lifting these bandages reeking of iodine
I plunged my hands in humble aches that would have
     smothered dying
and nothing did I meet within the wound save wind in gusts
that chilled my cold interstices of soul.

VI

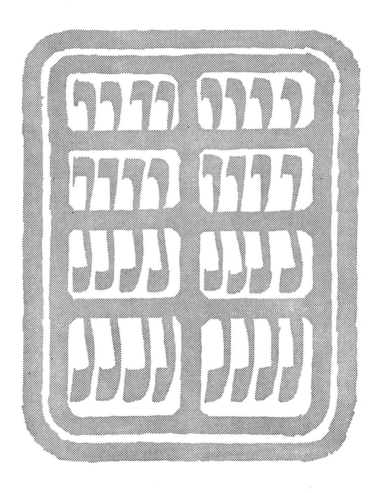

Entonces en la escala de la tierra he subido
entre la atroz maraña de las selvas perdidas
hasta ti, Macchu Picchu.

Alta ciudad de piedras escalares,
por fin morada del que lo terrestre
no escondió en las dormidas vestiduras.
En ti, como dos líneas paralelas,
la cuna del relámpago y del hombre
se mecían en un viento de espinas.

Madre de piedra, espuma de los cóndores.

Alto arrecife de la aurora humana.

Pala perdida en la primera arena.

Esta fué la morada, éste es el sitio:
aquí los anchos granos del maíz ascendieron
y bajaron de nuevo como granizo rojo.

Aquí la hebra dorada salió de la vicuña
a vestir los amores, los túmulos, las madres,
el rey, las oraciones, los guerreros.

THEN up the ladder of the earth I climbed
through the barbed jungle's thickets
until I reached you Macchu Picchu.

Tall city of stepped stone,
home at long last of whatever earth
had never hidden in her sleeping clothes.
In you two lineages that had run parallel
met where the cradle both of man and light
rocked in a wind of thorns.

Mother of stone and sperm of condors.

High reef of the human dawn.

Spade buried in primordial sand.

This was the habitation, this is the site:
here the fat grains of maize grew high
to fall again like red hail.

The fleece of the vicuña was carded here
to clothe men's loves in gold, their tombs and mothers,
the king, the prayers, the warriors.

Aquí los pies del hombre descansaron de noche
junto a los pies del águila, en las altas guaridas
carniceras, y en la aurora
pisaron con los pies del trueno la niebla enrarecida,
y tocaron las tierras y las piedras
hasta reconocerlas en la noche o la muerte.

Miro las vestiduras y las manos,
el vestigio del agua en la oquedad sonora,
la pared suavizada por el tacto de un rostro
que miró con mis ojos las lámparas terrestres,
que aceitó con mis manos las desaparecidas
maderas: porque todo, ropaje, piel, vasijas,
palabras, vino, panes,
se fué, cayó a la tierra.

Y el aire entró con dedos
de azahar sobre todos los dormidos:
mil años de aire, meses, semanas de aire,
de viento azul, de cordillera férrea,
que fueron como suaves huracanes de pasos
lustrando el solitario recinto de la piedra.

Up here men's feet found rest at night
near eagles' talons in the high
meat-stuffed eyries. And in the dawn
with thunder steps they trod the thinning mists,
touching the earth and stones that they might recognize
that touch come night, come death.

I gaze at clothes and hands,
traces of water in the booming cistern,
a wall burnished by the touch of a face
that witnessed with my eyes the earth's carpet of tapers,
oiled with my hands the vanished wood:
for everything, apparel, skin, pots, words,
wine, loaves, has disappeared,
fallen to earth.

And the air came in with lemon blossom fingers
to touch those sleeping faces:
a thousand years of air, months, weeks of air,
blue wind and iron cordilleras—
these came with gentle footstep hurricanes
cleansing the lonely precinct of the stone.

VII

MUERTOS *de un solo abismo, sombras de una hondonada,*
la profunda, es así como al tamaño
de vuestra magnitud
vino la verdadera, la más abrasadora
muerte y desde las rocas taladradas,
desde los capiteles escarlata,
desde los acueductos escalares
os desplomasteis como en un otoño
en una sola muerte.
Hoy el aire vacío ya no llora,
ya no conoce vuestros pies de arcilla,
ya olvidó vuestros cántaros que filtraban el cielo
cuando lo derramaban los cuchillos del rayo,
y el árbol poderoso fué comido
por la niebla, y cortado por la racha.
Él sostuvo una mano que cayó de repente
desde la altura hasta el final del tiempo.
Ya no sois, manos de araña, débiles
hebras, tela enmarañada:
cuanto fuiste cayó: costumbres, sílabas
raídas, máscaras de luz deslumbradora.

Pero una permanencia de piedra y de palabra:
la ciudad como un vaso se levantó en las manos
de todos, vivos, muertos, callados, sostenidos
de tanta muerte, un muro, de tanta vida un golpe

You dead of a common abyss, shades of one ravine—
the deepest—as if to match
the compass of your magnitude,
this is how it came, the true, the most consuming death:
from perforated rocks,
from crimson cornices,
and cataracting aqueducts,
you plummeted like an autumn
into a single death.
Today the vacant air no longer mourns
nor knows your shardlike feet,
forgets your pitchers that filtered the sky
when the knives of the lightning ripped it open
and the powerful tree was devoured
by mist and felled by wind.
It sustained a hand that suddenly pitched
from the heights to the depths of time.
You no longer exist: spider fingers, frail
threads, tangled cloth—everything you were
dropped away: customs and tattered
syllables, the dazzling masks of light.

And yet a permanence of stone and language
upheld the city raised like a chalice
in all those hands: live, dead and stilled,
aloft with so much death, a wall, with so much life,

de pétalos de piedra: la rosa permanente, la morada:
este arrecife andino de colonias glaciales.

Cuando la mano de color de arcilla
se convirtió en arcilla, y cuando los pequeños párpados se cerraron
llenos de ásperos muros, poblados de castillos,
y cuando todo el hombre se enredó en su agujero,
quedó la exactitud enarbolada:
el alto sitio de la aurora humana:
la más alta vasija que contuvo el silencio:
una vida de piedra después de tantas vidas.

struck with flint petals: the everlasting rose, our home,
this reef on Andes, its glacial territories.

On the day the clay-colored hand
was utterly changed into clay, and when dwarf eyelids closed
upon bruised walls and hosts of battlements,
when all of man in us cringed back into its burrow—
there remained a precision unfurled
on the high places of the human dawn,
the tallest crucible that ever held our silence,
a life of stone after so many lives.

VIII

Sube conmigo, *amor americano*.

Besa conmigo las piedras secretas.
La plata torrencial del Urubamba
hace volar el polen a su copa amarilla.
Vuela el vacío de la enredadera,
la planta pétrea, la guirnalda dura
sobre el silencio del cajón serrano.
Ven, minúscula vida, entre las alas
de la tierra, mientras—cristal y frío, aire golpeado—
apartando esmeraldas combatidas,
oh, agua salvaje, bajas de la nieve.

Amor, amor, hasta la noche abrupta,
desde el sonoro pedernal andino,
hacia la aurora de rodillas rojas,
contempla el hijo ciego de la nieve.

Oh, Wilkamayu de sonoros hilos,
cuando rompes tus truenos lineales
en blanca espuma, como herida nieve,
cuando tu vendaval acantilado
canta y castiga despertando al cielo,
qué idioma traes a la oreja apenas
desarraigada de tu espuma andina?

Come up with me, American love.

Kiss these secret stones with me.
The torrential silver of the Urubamba
makes the pollen fly to its golden cup.
The hollow of the bindweed's maze,
the petrified plant, the inflexible garland,
soar above the silence of these mountain coffers.
Come, diminutive life, between the wings
of the earth, while you, cold, crystal in the hammered air,
thrusting embattled emeralds apart,
O savage waters, fall from the hems of snow.

Love, love, until the night collapses
from the singing Andes flint
down to the dawn's red knees,
come out and contemplate the snow's blind son.

O Wilkamayu of the sounding looms,
when you rend your skeins of thunder
in white foam clouds of wounded snow,
when your south wind falls like an avalanche
roaring and belting to arouse the sky,
what language do you wake in an ear
freed but a moment from your Andean spume?

Quién apresó el relámpago del frío
y lo dejó en la altura encadenado,
repartido en sus lágrimas glaciales,
sacudido en sus rápidas espadas,
golpeando sus estambres aguerridos,
conducido en su cama de guerrero,
sobresaltado en su final de roca?

Qué dicen tus destellos acosados?
Tu secreto relámpago rebelde
antes viajó poblado de palabras?
Quién va rompiendo sílabas heladas,
idiomas negros, estandartes de oro,
bocas profundas, gritos sometidos,
en tus delgadas aguas arteriales?

Quién va cortando párpados florales
que vienen a mirar desde la tierra?
Quién precipita los racimos muertos
que bajan en tus manos de cascada
a desgranar su noche desgranada
en el carbón de la geología?

Quién despeña la rama de los vínculos?
Quién otra vez sepulta los adioses?

Who caught the lightning of the cold,
abandoned it, chained to the heights,
dealt out among its frozen tears,
brandished upon its nimble swords—
its seasoned stamens pummeled hard—
led to a warrior's bed,
hounded to his rocky conclusions?

What do your harried scintillations whisper?
Did your sly, rebellious flash
go traveling once, populous with words?
Who wanders grinding frozen syllables,
black languages, gold-threaded banners,
fathomless mouths and trampled cries
in your tenuous arterial waters?

Who goes dead-heading blossom eyelids
come to observe us from the far earth?
Who scatters dead seed clusters
dropping from your cascading hands
to bed their own disintegration here
in coal's geology?

Who has flung down the branches of these chains
and buried once again our leave-takings?

Amor, amor, no toques la frontera,
ni adores la cabeza sumergida:
deja que el tiempo cumpla su estatura
en su salón de manantiales rotos,
y, entre el agua veloz y las murallas,
recoge el aire del desfiladero,
las paralelas láminas del viento,
el canal ciego de las cordilleras,
el áspero saludo del rocío,
y sube, flor a flor, por la espesura,
pisando la serpiente despeñada.

En la escarpada zona, piedra y bosque,
polvo de estrellas verdes, selva clara,
Mantur estalla como un lago vivo
o como un nuevo piso del silencio.

Ven a mi propio ser, al alba mía,
hasta las soledades coronadas.

El reino muerto vive todavía.

Y en el Reloj la sombra sanguinaria
del cóndor cruza como una nave negra.

Love, love, do not come near the border,
avoid adoring this sunken head:
let time exhaust all measure
in its abode of broken overtures—
here, between cliffs and rushing waters,
take to yourself the air among these passes,
the laminated image of the wind,
the blind canal threading high cordilleras,
dew with its bitter greetings,
and climb, flower by flower, through the thicknesses
trampling the coiling lucifer.

In this steep zone of flint and forest,
green stardust, jungle-clarified,
Mantur, the valley, cracks like a living lake
or a new level of silence.

Come to my very being, to my own dawn,
into crowned solitudes.

The fallen kingdom survives us all this while.

And on this dial the condor's shadow
cruises as ravenous as would a pirate ship.

IX

ÁGUILA SIDERAL, *viña de bruma.*

Bastión perdido, cimitarra ciega.

Cinturón estrellado, pan solomne.

Escala torrencial, párpado inmenso.

Túnica triangular, polen de piedra.

Lámpara de granito, pan de piedra.

Serpiente mineral, rosa de piedra.

Nave enterrada, manantial de piedra.

Caballo de la luna, luz de piedra.

Escuadra equinoccial, vapor de piedra.

Geometría final, libro de piedra.

Témpano entre las ráfagas labrado.

Madrépora del tiempo sumergido.

Interstellar eagle, vine-in-a-mist.

Forsaken bastion, blind scimitar.

Orion belt, ceremonial bread.

Torrential stairway, immeasurable eyelid.

Triangular tunic, pollen of stone.

Granite lamp, bread of stone.

Mineral snake, rose of stone.

Ship-burial, source of stone.

Horse in the moon, stone light.

Equinoctial quadrant, vapor of stone.

Ultimate geometry, book of stone.

Iceberg carved among squalls.

Coral of sunken time.

Muralla por los dedos suavizada.

Techumbre por las plumas combatida.

Ramos de espejo, bases de tormenta.

Tronos volcados por la enredadera.

Régimen de la garra encarnizada.

Vendaval sostenido en la vertiente.

Inmóvil catarata de turquesa.

Campana patriarcal de los dormidos.

Argolla de las nieves dominadas.

Hierro acostado sobre sus estatuas.

Inaccesible temporal cerrado.

Manos de puma, roca sanguinaria.

Torre sombrera, discusión de nieve.

Finger-softened rampart.

Feather-assaulted roof.

Mirror splinters, thunderstorm foundations.

Thrones ruined by the climbing vine.

The blood-flecked talon's law.

Gale at a standstill on a slope.

Still turquoise cataract.

Patriarchal chiming of the sleepers.

Manacle of subjugated snows.

Iron tilting toward statues.

Storm inaccessible and closed.

Puma paws, bloodstone.

Towering shadow, convocation of snows.

Noche elevada en dedos y raíces.

Ventana de las nieblas, paloma endurecida.

Planta nocturna, estatua de los truenos.

Cordillera esencial, techo marino.

Arquitectura de águilas perdidas.

Cuerda del cielo, abeja de la altura.

Nivel sangriento, estrella construída.

Burbuja mineral, luna de cuarzo.

Serpiente andina, frente de amaranto.

Cúpula del silencio, patria pura.

Novia del mar, árbol de catedrales.

Ramo de sal, cerezo de alas negras.

Dentadura nevada, trueno frío.

Night hoisted upon fingers and roots.

Window of the mists, heartless dove.

Nocturnal foliage, icon of thunderclaps.

Cordillera spine, oceanic roof.

Architecture of stray eagles.

Sky rope, climax of the drone.

Blood level, constructed star.

Mineral bubble, moon of quartz.

Andean serpent, amaranthine brow.

Dome of silence, unsullied home.

Sea bride, cathedral timber.

Branch of salt, black-winged cherry tree.

Snowcapped teeth, chill thunder.

Luna arañada, piedra amenazante.

Cabellera del frío, acción del aire.

Volcán de manos, catarata oscura.

Ola de plata, dirección del tiempo.

Scarred moon, menacing stone.

Hair of the cold, friction of wind.

Volcano of hands, dark cataract.

Silver wave. Destination of time.

X

PIEDRA en la piedra, el hombre, dónde estuvo?
Aire en el aire, el hombre, dónde estuvo?
Tiempo en el tiempo, el hombre, dónde estuvo?
Fuiste también el pedacito roto
de hombre inconcluso, de águila vacía
que por las calles de hoy, que por las huellas,
que por las hojas del otoño muerto
va machacando el alma hasta la tumba?
La pobre mano, el pie, la pobre vida . . .
Los días de la luz deshilachada
en ti, como la lluvia
sobre las banderillas de la fiesta,
dieron pétalo a pétalo de su alimento oscuro
en la boca vacía?

        Hambre, coral del hombre,
hambre, planta secreta, raíz de los leñadores,
hambre, subió tu raya de arrecife
hasta estas altas torres desprendidas?

Yo te interrogo, sal de los caminos,
muéstrame la cuchara, déjame, arquitectura,
roer con un palito los estambres de piedra,
subir todos los escalones del aire hasta el vacío,
rascar la entraña hasta tocar el hombre.
Macchu Picchu, pusiste
piedras en la piedra, y en la base, harapo?

Sᴛᴏɴᴇ within stone, and man, where was he?
Air within air, and man, where was he?
Time within time, and man, where was he?
Were you also the shattered fragment
of indecision, of hollow eagle
which, through the streets of today, in the old tracks,
through the leaves of accumulated autumns,
goes pounding at the soul into the tomb?
Poor hand, poor foot, and poor, dear life . . .
The days of unraveled light
in you, familiar rain
falling on feast-day banderillas,
did they grant, petal by petal, their dark nourishment
to such an empty mouth?
                        Famine, coral of mankind,
hunger, secret plant, root of the woodcutters,
famine, did your jagged reef dart up
to those high, side-slipping towers?

l question you, salt of the highways,
show me the trowel; allow me, architecture,
to fret stone stamens with a little stick,
climb all the steps of air into the emptiness,
scrape the intestine until I touch mankind.
Macchu Picchu, did you lift
stone above stone on a groundwork of rags?

Carbón sobre carbón, y en el fondo la lágrima?
Fuego en el oro, y en él, temblando el rojo
goterón de la sangre?

Devuélveme el esclavo que enterraste!
Sacude de las tierras el pan duro
del miserable, muéstrame los vestidos
del siervo y su ventana.
Dime cómo durmió cuando vivía.
Dime si fué su sueño
ronco, entreabierto, como un hoyo negro
hecho por la fatiga sobre el muro.
El muro, el muro! Si sobre su sueño
gravitó cada piso de piedra, y si cayó bajo ella
como bajo una luna, con el sueño!

Antigua América, novia sumergida,
también tus dedos,
al salir de la selva hacia el alto vacío de los dioses,
bajo los estandartes nupciales de la luz y el decoro,
mezclándose al trueno de los tambores y de las lanzas,
también, también tus dedos,
los que la rosa abstracta y la línea del frío, los
que el pecho sangriento del nuevo cereal trasladaron
hasta la tela de materia radiante, hasta las duras cavidades,
también, también, América enterrada, guardaste en lo más bajo,
en el amargo intestino, como un águila, el hambre?

coal upon coal and, at the bottom, tears?
fire-crested gold, and in that gold, the bloat
dispenser of this blood?

Let me have back the slave you buried here!
Wrench from these lands the stale bread
of the poor, prove me the tatters
on the serf, point out his window.
Tell me how he slept when alive,
whether he snored,
his mouth agape like a dark scar
worn by fatigue into the wall.
That wall, that wall! If each stone floor
weighed down his sleep, and if he fell
beneath them, as if beneath a moon, with all that sleep!

Ancient America, bride in her veil of sea,
your fingers also,
from the jungle's edges to the rare height of gods,
under the nuptial banners of light and reverence,
blending with thunder from the drums and lances,
your fingers, your fingers also—
that bore the rose in mind and hairline of the cold,
the blood-drenched breast of the new crops translated
into the radiant weave of matter and adamantine hollows—
with them, with them, buried America, were you in that great depth,
the bilious gut, hoarding the eagle hunger?

XI

A TRAVÉS DEL *confuso esplendor,*
a través de la noche de piedra, déjame hundir la mano
y deja que en mí palpite, como un ave mil años prisionera,
el viejo corazón del olvidado!
Déjame olvidar hoy esta dicha, que es más ancha que el mar,
porque el hombre es más ancho que el mar y que sus islas,
y hay que caer en él como en un pozo para salir del fondo
con un ramo de agua secreta y de verdades sumergidas.
Déjame olvidar, ancha piedra, la proporción poderosa,
la trascendente medida, las piedras del panal,
y de la escuadra déjame hoy resbalar
la mano sobre la hipotenusa de áspera sangre y cilicio.

Cuando, como una herradura de élitros rojos, el cóndor furibundo
me golpea las sienes en el orden del vuelo
y el huracán de plumas carniceras barre el polvo sombrío
de las escalinatas diagonales, no veo a la bestia veloz,
no veo el ciego ciclo de sus garras,
veo el antiguo ser, servidor, el dormido
en los campos, veo un cuerpo, mil cuerpos, un hombre, mil mujeres,
bajo la racha negra, negros de lluvia y noche,
con la piedra pesada de la estatua:
Juan Cortapiedras, hijo de Wiracocha,
Juan Comefrío, hijo de estrella verde,
Juan Piesdescalzos, nieto de la turquesa,
sube a nacer conmigo, hermano.

Through a confusion of splendor,
through a night made stone let me plunge my hand
and move to beat in me a bird held for a thousand years,
the old and unremembered human heart!
Today let me forget this happiness, wider than all the sea,
because man is wider than all the sea and her necklace of islands
and we must fall into him as down a well to clamber back with
branches of secret water, recondite truths.
Allow me to forget, circumference of stone, the powerful
    proportions,
the transcendental span, the honeycomb's foundations,
and from the set-square allow my hand to slide
down a hypotenuse of hairshirt and salt blood.

When, like a horseshoe of rusting wing-cases, the furious condor
batters my temples in the order of flight
and his tornado of carnivorous feathers sweeps the dark dust
down slanting stairways, I do not see the rush of the bird,
nor the blind sickle of his talons—
I see the ancient being, the slave, the sleeping one,
blanket his fields—a body, a thousand bodies, a man, a thousand
women swept by the sable whirlwind, charred with rain and night,
stoned with a leaden weight of statuary:
Juan Splitstones, son of Wiracocha,
Juan Coldbelly, heir of the green star,
Juan Barefoot, grandson to the turquoise,
rising to birth with me, as my own brother.

XII

Sube a nacer *conmigo, hermano.*

Dame la mano desde la profunda
zona de tu dolor diseminado.
No volverás del fondo de las rocas.
No volverás del tiempo subterráneo.
No volverá tu voz endurecida.
No volverán tus ojos taladrados.

Mírame desde el fondo de la tierra,
labrador, tejedor, pastor callado:
domador de guanacos tutelares:
albañil del andamio desafiado:
aguador de las lágrimas andinas:
joyero de los dedos machacados:
agricultor temblando en la semilla:
alfarero en tu greda derramado:
traed a la copa de esta nueva vida
vuestros viejos dolores enterrados.
Mostradme vuestra sangre y vuestro surco,
decidme: aquí fuí castigado,
porque la joya no brilló o la tierra
no entregó a tiempo la piedra o el grano:
señaladme la piedra en que caísteis

ARISE TO BIRTH with me, my brother.

Give me your hand out of the depths
sown by your sorrows.
You will not return from these stone fastnesses.
You will not emerge from subterranean time.
Your rasping voice will not come back,
nor your pierced eyes rise from their sockets.

Look at me from the depths of the earth,
tiller of fields, weaver, reticent shepherd,
groom of totemic guanacos,
mason high on your treacherous scaffolding,
iceman of Andean tears,
jeweler with crushed fingers,
farmer anxious among his seedlings,
potter wasted among his clays—
bring to the cup of this new life
your ancient buried sorrows.
Show me your blood and your furrow;
say to me: here I was scourged
because a gem was dull or because the earth
failed to give up in time its tithe of corn or stone.
Point out to me the rock on which you stumbled,

y la madera en que os crucificaron,
encendedme los viejos pedernales,
las viejas lámparas, los látigos pegados
a través de los siglos en las llagas
y las hachas de brillo ensangrentado.

Yo vengo a hablar por vuestra boca muerta.

A través de la tierra juntad todos
los silenciosos labios derramados
y desde el fondo habladme toda esta larga noche,
como si yo estuviera con vosotros anclado.

Contadme todo, cadena a cadena,
eslabón a eslabón, y paso a paso,
afilad los cuchillos que guardasteis,
ponedlos en mi pecho y en mi mano,
como un río de rayos amarillos,
como un río de tigres enterrados,
y dejadme llorar, horas, días, años,
edades ciegas, siglos estelares.

the wood they used to crucify your body.
Strike the old flints
to kindle ancient lamps, light up the whips
glued to your wounds throughout the centuries
and light the axes gleaming with your blood.

I come to speak for your dead mouths.

Throughout the earth
let dead lips congregate,
out of the depths spin this long night to me
as if I rode at anchor here with you.

And tell me everything, tell chain by chain,
and link by link, and step by step;
sharpen the knives you kept hidden away,
thrust them into my breast, into my hands,
like a torrent of sunbursts,
an Amazon of buried jaguars,
and leave me cry: hours, days and years,
blind ages, stellar centuries.

Dadme el silencio, el agua, la esperanza.

Dadme la lucha, el hierro, los volcanes.

Apegadme los cuerpos como imanes.

Acudid a mis venas y a mi boca.

Hablad por mis palabras y mi sangre.

And give me silence, give me water, hope.

Give me the struggle, the iron, the volcanoes.

Let bodies cling like magnets to my body.

Come quickly to my veins and to my mouth.

Speak through my speech, and through my blood.